A BEAUTIFUL HELL

A BEAUTIFUL HELL

poems by

Carol Kapaun Ratchenski

Many Voices Project #133

Cover and interior design by Briana Schepper
Author photo by Taylor Made Photography

The publication of *A Beautiful Hell* is made possible by the generous support of Minnesota State University Moorhead, The McKnight Foundation, the Dawson Family Endowment, and other generous contributors to New Rivers Press.

For copyright permission, please contact Frederick T. Courtright at 570-839-7447 or permdude@eclipse.net.

New Rivers Press is a nonprofit literary press associated with Minnesota State University Moorhead.

Alan Davis, Director and Senior Editor
Nayt Rundquist, Managing Editor
Kevin Carollo, MVP Poetry Coordinator
Bayard Godsave, MVP Prose Coordinator
Thom Tammro, Poetry Editor
Thomas Anstadt, Co-Art Director
Trista Conzemius, Co-Art Director
Wayne Gudmundson, Consultant
Suzzanne Kelley, Consultant

Publishing Interns:
Laura Grimm, Anna Landsverk, Desiree Miller, Mikaila Norman

A Beautiful Hell book team:
Brittany Densmore, Shelly Sibley

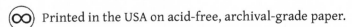 Printed in the USA on acid-free, archival-grade paper.

A Beautiful Hell is distributed nationally by Small Press Distribution.

 New Rivers Press
c/o MSUM
1104 7th Avenue South
Moorhead, MN 56563
www.newriverspress.com

For

David and Adam Ratchenski and Amy Kapaun, this is ours.
And in memory of my grandmothers, Helen and Lizzy, I am yours.

CONTENTS

Sailor Mom 1

Sing Along 2

Raffle Ticket 4

Rivers and Light 6

Real Healing 7

Please Put This in His Chart 8

A Tale 9

Premonition 11

Bad News: A Friendship 12

Julio: Short Order Cook in Hell, Mayo Clinic, 1999 14

Women of the New Testament 15

Night Nurse 16

Color of Freedom 17

Choices 18

Nursing Father 19

Our Cruise 20

There, There, or Something Better 21

Disturbances in the Field 23

Divine One-Way 24

Walking Around It 25

Inspiration for Sale 26

Father's Day 27

The Grandmother Verses 28

Big Sale Today 34

Unmothering 36

Only Child 39

What Remains 40

Mothers United 41

Gravy, High Heels 42

Mess 44

The Worst Loss 46

Evidence 47

Counting 48

Icy Roads 51

Defiant Gardeners 52

Compatriots: Columbine and Red Lake 54

Second Born 55

The Hairpiece 56

Later in Nashville 58

The Reading Cure 59

Time Clock Cure 60

Unwatched 61

Condolences 62

Sunday Driving 63

Acknowledgments
About the Author
About New Rivers Press

"Hard times require furious dancing. Each of us is the proof."
—Alice Walker

Sailor Mom

I swore at my babies. Like a sailor-mom. It is not the parenting behavior I am proudest of, but my sisters will tell you if I don't. I walked them in the middle of the night, teething or fevering with earaches and in the sweetest most nurturing voice you could imagine I swore at my babies. It helped me and they were pre-language, aware only of tone and touch. I was gentle at both and profane. Even after his diagnosis, I didn't stop though I tried then, because I was ashamed and thought his illness might even be the result of such harsh words in his tender membrane ears. If in the new age I am responsible for my reality, then surely my foul mouth could have grown black tumor cells in his brain. At four in the morning, this made sense and I swore anyway. Too tired to censor, craving sleep more than long life for either of us. Medicine to give every two hours, portable IV hydration, a grotesque backpack for toddlers needing round-the-clock chemotherapy drugs, new obscenities every day. Swearing helped: red wine and a pinch or two of his medical marijuana over my oatmeal. I don't apologize. Fuck the new age.

Sing Along

I push my two-year-old in his stroller,
His head smooth from the chemotherapy,
Over the broken sidewalk on Front Street.
My grandpa's childhood home stood here
Before they tore it down to put up the new fire hall.
As we pass the tall steel doors and red "No Parking" signs,
We listen for the tinkling keys, a xylophone cord,
A melody from Frank Sinatra, the perfect interior rhyme
Of Mahalia Jackson or Hank Williams.

Music like cancer runs in our family.
Deep and random.

I tell my son that his great-grandpa loved the snare drum
Post-war American dance halls, unfiltered Camels and
The soft, moist red hair on the back of my grandma's neck.
I teach him to listen closely to his history, and mine.
Every note, every word is still here somewhere, I assure him.
This was the kind of three-generational household
We can be romantic about, far as we are
From the bitter disputes around kitchen rituals and spices,
And the high tax familiarity takes on respect.

My mother was proud to take my Aunt Gerdie's place at the piano
After leukemia took her life at twenty-two.

My son will never know my mother.
She is dead decades before his birth.
My sister Melanie the only piano player he has ever known.
He loves to count the frets on my mandolin and his daddy's guitar,
Run his tongue along the smooth strings when he thinks we're not looking.
He has a basket of maracas, bells, cymbals, and mallets
That Melanie brought to the hospital soon after his diagnosis.
He played them all shamelessly loud until the nurses complained
And I took all but one yarned mallet home.

Back in his own bed, between treatments and infections,
He sleeps with that basket of noise.

Rattle, boom, chime at four in the morning.
If he's still playing, then he's still breathing.
Later we will take our morning walk. Stop at the Dairy Queen
For breakfast, hot chocolate malted milks.
We'll sit on the city park bench where his daddy first kissed me.
It was the spring of 1976, the country a big birthday party
And us ready to graduate high school, leave home, change everything.
My son will not drink much of his slippery treat so I finish it for him.
A soupy reminder of sweetness that becomes something else.

His feet stomping on the stroller footrest, we'll sing
"I'm so lonesome I could cry," fierce and off-key all the way home.

Raffle Ticket

He was beautiful. And tall and well dressed. Lovely shoes. But all this isn't why I trusted him with my son's life, twice. Said yes, do surgery. Remove the tumor that makes him fall over when he tries to walk, that makes him tilt his head to the left. No one would notice, not even a mother, but always just a bit off center. His name was Dr. Corey Raffle. Like the way you buy a ticket for cheap and hope for the big prize. His beauty made me feel lucky, a good sign, a pediatric neurosurgeon who looks like Jesus at the end of the twentieth century. I said yes and waited for him to come tell me that it was over, Kevin was okay. They may have gotten it all. It's reasonable to hope for that. Remembering that cancer is like ink in sand, not a beach ball buried and just waiting to pop out wholly released and intact. Uncontainable sticky liquid death. And he had worse news for me. Neuroblastoma, under five percent survival, stage four. My son was two years old, and two days earlier I thought he was a healthy, normal-growing child with a lingering flu bug. Now I had a ticket to another planet and this modern-day Jesus to teach me a language I didn't want to learn. Whole-brain radiation therapy. It could save him but leave him a permanent toddler. His body might grow, but his brain wouldn't develop any further than this lovely trusting place. Lovely because it doesn't last but passes into concrete operations and teenage angst and young adulthood, middle age, and if we're lucky, gentle late life. Stronger people than me, says Jesus, do this. I wouldn't sentence my son to terminal toddlerhood. Or I wouldn't sentence myself to care of a disabled son, no empty nest for me ever, only caretaking ahead. If Jesus couldn't do it how could I, a good enough mother before and after work, which took me away to days of stimulating adult conversation while other women watched Sesame Street and ate macaroni and cheese with my sons. Marys all of them. Stronger than Jesus, so much less fame, so much more godlike. Over the nine months that my son's cancer gestated, Dr. Jesus said many things to me: Get some sleep. Don't use the internet to try to understand this. I went to medical school for both of us. But his most important gospel, spoken weeks before this mothering planet opened up to hold my son forever, death isn't the enemy, cancer is the enemy, and cancer never wins.

Rivers and Light

I recommend nephrologists. Get one if you can. Take one for a lover, a friend, a husband. Angels and saints disguised as kidney doctors. The hidden eighth sacrament. With knee-length white to cover wings and magic called dialysis for communion. Of all the professionals who studied my son, his chart, his blood, his PET scans and reflexes, only these chanted love verses, held his mere twenty pounds on their own laps, kissed his scarred head with their eyes closed, prayed and called at three in the morning, knowing we would be awake for blood draws, called because there's a barge on the river. Look out to the east. Goddamn lights on it like a gypsy Christmas tree. Tell Kevin it's for him. Tell him God's cramming heaven into His earth everywhere. Just for him.

Real Healing

Real healers don't have degrees. No initials behind their formally displayed names. Or white coats or Mercedes Benz keys. No access to narcotics by a sprawl of illegible letters. No reserved parking spaces or beepers or lake homes. Real healers punch a grey time clock, carry plaid lunch pails, and save for Christmas accounts and two week road trips to the Black Hills over the Fourth of July every other year. Real healers notice when Kevin wears the new green scrubs that Grandma bought in the gift shop downstairs and that I drink coffee at night and Diet Coke in the mornings.

Real healers tell us an elephant joke when they empty the garbage can filled with toxic waste without gloves. Diapers, Kleenex, and straws he has used within seventy-two hours of chemotherapy. Real healers wear Kevin's favorite smiley face earrings for months after they make him laugh one day when he could sit up and mouth the word happy around his infected gums and rotting baby teeth. Real healers smuggle grape popsicles in their faded smock pockets when they transport Kevin, me, and his growing chart between endless identical hallways leading to EKG, MRI, and CAT scan rooms.

A real healer, in the hour and a half between delivering breakfast and lunch trays, smuggles a talking Winnie the Pooh to us on a scary Sunday when Kevin's oxygen and platelets were both low, blood on the way but he hates the tubes that might help him breathe. Smuggled because she could be fired—but her own daughter is just Kevin's age and she too loves the song about honey. Therefore, Kevin, she tells me, is her child too. I never see her again. I never know if she was found out and fired for loving my son, sent home for being a real healer in a world that was day by day giving up on healing my son.

Please Put This in His Chart

No traveling nurses. No residents. No student nurses. No grand rounds without me present. If he wants to sleep on the floor let him. If he wants to be carried carry him. He calls wheelchairs fancy chairs. If he wants to go fast, go fast. If he wants to go outside, take him outside. If he wants junk food, give it to him. Order out and I'll pay you back. He calls his brother that guy. If he wants to call his brother, dial for him. If he wants his grandma, call her, send a taxi, I'll pay you back the fare. No blood draws without his permission. He will always let you draw from his portable catheter. Use it whenever you can. If you take his blood pressure, let him take yours. Kiss him goodnight. I'll be in the bathroom praying or in the chapel throwing up.

A Tale

It was the best of times, it was the worst of times. I know I borrowed that line and I'm not sure if it is two sentences or a run on. Still, it's perfect. And I worry about this more than anything. That this one defining thing you won't believe. It was the best year of my life. That most clear, shiny time of all. If this is the land and the time of choices, then the joy came to me when all my options disappeared. Madison Avenue and Wall Street and perhaps you don't want to hear this. One change of clothes, no earrings, no perfume, no other shoes, no other shampoo. Just these. I don't wonder what goes with this or that. There is no this, no that. No two concerts to pick between, no similar restaurants to choose among, no matinee versus evening showing. Just this. Blood draw at seven and MRI at noon. Nourishment in between and again after. Nap. Doctor rounds at four. Dinner at six. Blood pressure check every twenty minutes, twenty-four hours a day. Wagon rides and wheelchair let go down ramps and caught just in time. Laughter. Strong coffee-flavored coffee, real maple syrup, and dark chocolate. Deep sleepless nights and dreamless naps. The familiarity of rotating nurses and other uniformed lovers. The sameness, the numbers, one over another, we measure platelets and temperature. Quantifying mystery, his, not mine. I count how many steps I take in a day. I drink eight glasses of water until I pee clear, simple signs of health in my body. The nurses tell me early on that it will be important to keep the pronouns clear. I do not have cancer or chemotherapy in the morning. I do not have a portable catheter in my chest or in my groin. I find Barney obscenely irritating and I shower every day. When Kevin discovers the squealing Telletubbies, I long for the big purple guy like I will later yearn for him, next to me in bed, behind me or beside me in some contraption I pull or push or drag. Like all longing, it becomes nostalgic and therefore euphoric and sweet. It was not a minimalist, but cozy ashram for two. Sharp needles and four percent survival rates do not add up to blissful Midwestern Zen, no matter how many of my friends have since gone east for peace. Still white hallways between the sleeping, the time before dying, the pure being of living while dying—all a better rest than most of us will ever know, the fierce and gentle peace of paradox, the only real rest for the living.

Premonition

It's one of those things that I can only tell after and yet it is meaningless because I didn't tell it before. Three weeks before I first heard the word neuroblastoma, first looked at my son as a sick child, for twenty-one days I didn't sleep. I tossed and paced and read horrible novels into the night. Ten days into this famous but new to me form of torture, I went to my family doctor and begged for sleeping pills, and because I wasn't a regular self-diagnoser, self-prescriber, she gave me a script and I closed my eyes to the dark and dreamt. When I woke up somewhere between here and there, I heard my own voice say, "Someone in this house has a brain tumor." Of course I was convinced it was me and took to hugging my kids longer and making love with my eyes on my husband's lovely face harder. Tried not to cry in either situation so as not to scare them all. Played the brave patient, grateful for all I've had and yet not clinging for more than my share. But I couldn't do it. I was a grasper from the start. I'd been left a hundred times by then, by my mother and my father and nameless boyfriends who couldn't hurt me, tough orphan that I was by then. Me doing the leaving scared the shit out of me and I screamed into my pillow at night until my throat was raw and I began to drown out Kevin's cries in the night and pleas in the morning. Head hurt head hurt mama head hurt. I hope he knew how ready I was to leave. How willing I was to go instead or with him, how I expected to go, startled even to wake up at all that first year as a mother of one again, a few pills to spare, and my body still around my soul.

Bad News: A Friendship

I should have known when the pediatric clinic nurses started hugging me. I was on my way across town, to the hospital, the imaging department, not across an ocean or a sea, though that would have been less dramatic. They really have no license to touch, but without looking me in the eye they held me too long, too hard. But I knew nothing, lulled into complacency by the low infant mortality rates, good nutritional habits, and the general safety of middle North America at the end of the last century. Tornadoes the most dangerous possibility, hardly a worry this late in the fall.

They gave him some Versed, just enough to induce the afternoon nap he needed but didn't want. I stood beside him as the white tubular machine covered his head over and over. I was without earplugs, still a novice. I carried him to the pediatric ward to wait for the sedative to wear off, rocked him, thinking of his two-year-old birthday party the night before. His grandma yelling to me from the family room. "Kevin is walking around like he's drunk." My trying to remember if I gave him too much Motrin, his fever back again with no sign of strep or ear ache. His dad here by now, dressed from work and my sister up from the cardiac floor, where she is on the day shift. When the phone in the room rings, I am startled. Wrong number. Another family's call coming too late, after check out time if they call it that here. My husband answers and drops his face into his hands, drops the phone to the floor, where it bounces on its springy cord. I lean over to grab it, scream no into the phone, hear the breaking voice of our doctor, a mass, a tumor, bad news, stay where you are. Over and over, the only word I have, no, no, no, no, no, no. A dead line. The room begins to fill then, more nurses, smocks with cookie monster and jellybeans and faded rainbows. They are offering me coffee, juice, toast, anything at all, telling me we will be staying the night for observation. Surgery tomorrow, in another state, air ambulance, a phone card to use for whoever we need to call.

I dial my sisters, my brother, pray to my parents long since in heaven, leave messages at work and with my best friend's husband. LeeAnn lives 100 miles north of this hospital room with her two sons and a husband we have begun to worry about a lot, his depression turned lately to angry outbursts, furniture thrown, small appliances broken against walls and door frames, just over her head, just to the right of the high chair. He says he will tell her, page her if she's left the office already, she'll call me, and come on the weekend maybe. But he doesn't tell her. He tells their son, five years old at the time, that Kevin is dying and this child told his mom over soggy Captain Crunch a few days later. And both Kevin and her husband are dead before I hear the northern side of this story. It wasn't a broken bone or even a promise exactly, but it was a breaking, a destruction, an ending. The universe tilting us all. Still none of us knew it would kill her husband, this omission, this killing off of my son, newly diagnosed, still so full of hope with no scars yet to hide.

Julio: Short Order Cook in Hell, Mayo Clinic, 1999

He made eye contact with me even on the worst-news days. The days no one else would, for fear of my fear. What do you need this morning, darling? No matter he called everyone that, I let it in my dry heart, because he didn't look away from my grey face. Unlike the series of interns, nurses, and other gruesome technicians who didn't want what I had to offer. The cold shock of death living in a child's body. The mother who pushed him from her soft body once, now both of us so full of the short future. I smile fully and say wild mushroom omelet, whole wheat pancake, real maple syrup, hash browns with onions and garlic; today I need heavy, believable food. He listens and nods, never blinking, half-smile of a Yogi. He knows he can't help but offers what he can. I accept my warm oatmeal-colored plate as if communion, knowing it is holy, knowing he may be the only one here who can heal me. And I don't resist the urge to lick my sticky plate when it's empty, cross myself with maple fingers, the gesture of my ancestors, a way to keep Saint Julio with me all day long.

Women Of The New Testament

Gail Roen called me, by calling the nurses' station, St. Mary's Hospital Pediatric Intensive Care Unit. A nurse came to get me from my son's room. He was scarless, pre-surgery, if he was confused about the room, the machines connected to his chest, he didn't have a way to tell me. He still used a pacifier, loved the wheel chair ramps that his stroller sped down, the choirs that came to sing Christmas carols. Didn't notice my tears to songs of joy and praise. Gail had been my counselor, my mentor, and my friend. Fuzzy boundaries that abound in my field. She was blonde, wild, single, Jungian, and I sometimes imagined her as my real mother, separated at birth or lost to me in the bardo somewhere when my mother grabbed me, pulled me through, now long-dead when I needed more pulling. Think of the women of the Old Testament, Gail is saying. I am crying, so happy to hear her voice, to not be forgotten by that invisible generation that was my parents. Think of Easter, think of Lazarus's sisters, think of Rachel, oh fuck it, I forgot, you're Catholic, you never read the Bible, okay think of me, think of Dean Martin, think of Carol Burnett, think of Archie Bunker.

Night Nurse

She came in square and stern and black in crumpled green scrubs, her hands a huge wingspan when she held her arms out over my son's hospital bed. A blessing, a conductor, a warning. I am the mean night nurse, and here are the rules: only one visitor at a time, no touching him, no sleeping in the chair, if you're here make yourself useful stay out of my way, and pray. Mom you look like shit. You are banned from this room for the night. Go sleep somewhere. You all might be his family, but you're not my responsibility, so don't ask me where the pop machine is or who delivers pizza all night. You won't hear my voice again, and I don't want to hear yours. This boy is sick, and I intend to care for him like the angel I am. Tomorrow night we won't have to go through all this again.

Color of Freedom

My two year old son died with Purple Passionflower polish on his toes and fingernails. As soon as he could ask for something, at six months, pointing and grunting his intentions for food, drink, me, and dazzle on his toes, I painted him to match me. Not a daughter, but this at least we had in common early on, and it made me sigh with joy to greet him in the middle of the night, his Sunset Orange fingers held my breast to his mouth as his Firefly Red toes danced with satisfaction against my still-swollen stomach. Once, a colleague of my husband's laughed when he saw our sons and their Neon Punk Pink toes, made some homophobic joke that no one laughed at. The next day, my husband painted his own toes Deeply Madly Maroon and took his socks off at work and I knew I would never leave him in this lifetime. After my son's last breath, my husband asked me if I was going to take off the polish before we carried his body to our van and then into the local funeral home. Off his fingers, not his toes. I would not take that much of his dignity away in death. His life meant something, and some days, freedom needs all its champions shouting at once.

Choices

I am a child in the land of obscene choices. 109 television stations and more radio and blogs and chat rooms and eleven careers in one and choose your hair color and change your name if you want. We get to choose. No longer only three jobs for middle class girls, now a nameless number, invent your own degree program. Write a grant, create a job for yourself. No geographical limits. Colleagues in New York City and me on this farm. Way too many cold cereals to choose from and crackers by the hundreds. Flavors of coffee and chips and pasta. Then a year of respite. And peace descended on me, at last. Two changes of clothes in my suitcase, a watch, comfortable shoes, borrowed socks. My hair grew longer, and I got used to my face without makeup and my ears without earrings, my legs hairy and my coffee black and unflavored like my grandparents drank it, grateful for the warmth and bitterness in the morning. Something to let a person know they are alive, willing and available to meet the Lord, but grateful too for smaller concerns today, the wild oats taking over the barley and the calf coming too soon. A morning blood draw and a chest x-ray after lunch. Plenty of time to watch the elevators come and go, to watch for a barge on the Mississippi River out the family room window. Two recliners, side by side, our shared joy on spotting a robin, a crane, a hummingbird all in one week. Our only choice to watch some more. No chemotherapy until Tuesday, and if his blood pressure doesn't spike today, we'll cross the street in the morning for an Egg McMuffin and more black coffee. And we'll be glad to be back on the floor later with no decisions to make until tomorrow, when one of us must say yes or no to whole-brain radiation.

Nursing Father

St. Mary's Hospital Pediatric Intensive Care Unit, Tom, a male nurse and the father of twin boys, just Kevin's age, two-nearing-three years. He showed me pictures, trusting me not to hate him or these smiling dark faces with too much curly brown hair, plump and unaware of their same silly outfits. Two of a kind. I tried not to see it as one extra, a spare. Tom loved Kevin. Kissed him good night and told him so. Inappropriate and necessary and right. We talked about old remedies for earaches and teething woes, the magic of warm washcloths and salt water. At three in the morning, he told me how they were a surprise, imagine that, him a nurse and surprised. I told him that Kevin was a surprise too, not planned or even imagined, and right somehow. Right to be the mother of two. Perfect not to ask my older son to be an only, spoiled by the missed chance to learn how to share the planet from the beginning. Something his sons would never not know, having shared a womb, a cord of blood and food, two breasts and this father who dared to love my son knowing he, like me, would lose him.

Our Cruise

She knew it wasn't a crime or even a sin. Not an injustice or wrong. She went on a cruise, and I went down to x-ray, across to chemo, and out to lunch, which I mostly threw up. She wore colored sarongs and drank too much tequila and danced with boys half her age and slept all day in a deck chair ordering crab cakes and iced tea and drinks with umbrellas that she tucked behind her sunburned ears. Then she came home and took the elevator to the fourth floor, the rows of bald children and endless laundry, smells of vomit and Ensure and signs warning of radioactive waste. She knocked and banged her way into my son's hospital room. Carrying four shopping bags, her face peeling now, vacation flaking off and landing on these tile floors so used to worse offerings. She brought back painted wooden puppets and grass skirts, rattles and carved Buddhas made of ivory, soap, marble, and chewing gum. For her children and grandchildren and neighbors at the apartment building. But first she brought it all here for Kevin and me. Color and sound and twenty rolls of film. Blue ocean and white sand. Handsome waiters and buffets the size of football fields. She demonstrated the dance of island pelicans and the beach drummer's chants. She worked up a sweat and the three of us laughed and rattled and twirled in grass neither Kevin nor I will ever see. The world so big we didn't need to cry over it.

There, There, or Something Better

I am doing laps around the cemetery years later. The grass filled in on my son's grave as fully as on my mother's. Without the dates, no one would know how dead she was for how long before he was born. Ten years, one hundred and twenty months, I count the distance in toddler years. Of course, I was in my twenties when we buried her here. Moved out, married, degreed, long distance between us.

I walk around once, jog twice, walk another. In my ear, a cassette tape on relationships plays. I half listen for my work with couples in crisis and half for myself, also one half of a marriage that I can't seem to want to be in for more than a few hours running. All my training in family therapy doesn't help me know if this is alarming or common. Discernment is something I long for, and put off for the second half of my life, which is years away. Five if I live as long as my grandmother. Two if I live as long as the national average. And fourteen years behind me if I follow my mother, dead at fifty-two. It would be years before I knew she died young. Such is the blindness of youth and red wine. Death remains a dream no matter how near the knocking.

Now, stretching and sweating on the dewy grass, the lecture in my ear turns to heaven. "The first thing everyone sees," says the gentle speaker, "is whatever was their greatest comfort on Earth." I sink from downward dog pose to my knees, child's pose, my forehead pressing into the cold wet green. Dropped by the idea of Winnie the Pooh or me greeting him. And then unquietly, knowing for certain that she knew no comfort on the Earthly plane. No untortured sleep, no days without a fist or two of her own hair to flush away in shame. Full of cold coffee and rerun cop shows, her attempts at warmth, so failed.

Crawling to her stone, I know that this is her first sight of heaven. This grey stone with her fading name and dates, her children's names below. This sure sign of completion, release, peace in finishing, peace at last.

Disturbances in the Field

(For Jaden Donald Lemar)

You might have heard it in the movies or on cable. Ghosts cause electrical disturbances. Lights to flicker, clocks to lie, stoves to burn or refuse to cook.We've had a few, I say when asked. Mostly battery-operated toys that sing and signal in the night. Mournful songs or victory sounds wake me up and I roll over, return to what's left for me of sleep. That's another disturbed field, I suppose, having given up sleep for so many lunar cycles, I can ask for it back, but the dreamy gap doesn't open on request. So I nod off and read and pace and drink all forms of chamomile tea, burn my tongue, pace some more, roll around, sort socks, and check my e-mail. My nephew born just a season before Kevin has the most of it. My sister finds him awake in the middle of the night, out of bed playing with toys and video games and blocks and, he says, with Kevin. So she leaves him to it. He is undisturbed. If invisible friends are a normal part of development, just another phase of concrete relations establishing itself, what will this playmate do to his intellectual growth and world view? I pray it will do more than set him apart. That it might open possibilities usually hidden to the so young and hopefully protected. I wish mostly that my sweet nephew, always a reminder of what size my son might have been this year, will hold the mystery into his adult serious years, will always believe so easily, because he, like me, sleeps so little.

Divine One-Way

People cry in cars. Mostly when they're alone, sniffling, wiping their noses on their sleeve occasionally, and mostly at stop signs, pounding their heads on the not-so-soft leather of the steering wheel. If you haven't noticed yet, it's only because you're still on your cell phone, yelling at the talk radio host, or taking in more calories than most of the world will see this week, or all three. Or maybe you haven't been broken in two yet, assaulted by the knowledge that you could lose something you thought it would kill you to lose and it didn't. You are still here, expected at the dentist and baby shower and even at work. Expected to stop at red and yield at yellow, to make enough deposits in the karma bank of driving to make a reckless withdrawal now and then. Look both ways and then back again like everyone else and with a blurry Monet-like vision, through the tears and the slurping of mucus, you begin to wonder at the messy human animal, so wet and sticky, so goddamn resilient, and, you begin to suspect, capable of complete transcendence of belief and experience, capable of falling directly into the arms of something bigger, something stranger. A higher power, the universal field, mother/father god, holy ghost, the unspeakable thing that shatters disbelief when you survive the un-survivable, walk away without a visible scratch, and to your own astonishment, wake up craving decent coffee and the Sunday book section.

Walking Around It

I live across the street from our town's cemetery. Closer to the protestant side than the Catholic though I have more visiting to do on Mary's side. A sweet flowery labyrinth. I walk in it in the morning and after dark, circle by my grandma Lizzy and her husband I never knew and her dead babies and my parents and my own name listed under "parents of," as if that were their main concern. A sand hill crane carved above my father's name and a rose for my mom who hated roses, their thorns and dying ways and now here she is and forever. I come around twice on my route, once by the altar with headstones of priests and one witch who was married to a deacon and so gets to lie here too, and once through the evergreens and past my sister's dead boyfriend. A mountain road and a prairie boy far from flat, safe home. I don't pray for him anymore. Now I pray for his mother, still alive and tending the dark green military stone. I cross the line of faith in intercession and limbo to the less festive protestant acres, quickly to avoid the mosquitos and the feelings of treason that follow me. Here my other, sterner grandmother rests with her musician husband and only son. And a little to the east, my youngest son. I can walk past now without my knees giving way or my stomach releasing the day's gifts. I can water the flowers his grandpa plants with my hands steady and my eyes dry. I am no longer surprised to find my name again this time after "son of." As if that were his main concern. Years have filled in the grass and evened the ground and the spaces around his heart-shaped stone wait mostly patiently for my husband's parents, my husband, my sisters and the husbands they haven't divorced yet, and me. My surviving son will have to have a different plan, with his aged wife perhaps or flung out over a river or favorite hunting or fishing spot. It was too much like giving in to count him in on this plot, like asking my husband to stop smoking now when he so needs to die next, like asking me to have another child and not name it replacement, like asking my oldest son not to act like an only child, spoiled and protected and always a little bit guilty of something he can't name.

Inspiration for Sale

The autumn that this earth became to me the untrustworthy place it has always been, I tried to write something about this mother's grief that would fit on an inspirational poster. Something that might sell well at craft shows, off the back of a pick-up trailer. Cheap, for all their wisdom, really, a string of clichés that rhyme with Jesus and grace and bullshit. Words come to me from somewhere in the middle of a stuffed animal that still smells like my dead son or the hospital or both. I pull it lengthwise to my chest and it's the right size, but too light, even by the end, his weight diminished and I couldn't hold him anyway because his head hurt and I could never be as still as the sofa or later the bed that took up most of our living room, diagonally so I could stay in the recliner, read all the bookshelves around us on three sides, top to bottom, back again, then in Spanish, then in German, when I thought I would lose all touch with reality if I stayed in my mother tongue, this central time zone and my dull Midwestern monotone conversations. If Jesus wasn't born to please us and grace will find its own pace and don't push it by calling it all bullshit maybe I can save up all these crumpled singles, fill up with unleaded and make it to Austin by snowfall after all.

Father's Day

My friends mourn
Hardest in the spring
Father's day and mother's day
Before that.
But every day is kids' day
That's what my dad used to say
As he opened his presents
A few weeks after my mom's turn
Even as a child I could see
He was something less than
Grateful
Needing nothing
Loving nothing.
A blue-collar
I-shower-after-work
Kind of guy
Gave me a cruel gift—
An anniversary
Every day but two each year.
And mother's day harder yet
No presents for me
No school-made sloppy
Love notes
My Mother's Day flowers
Dying on a Memorial Day wreath
Hung on a lamb
Posed for prayer in marble
Over my son's scarred head.

The Grandmother Verses

I

My grandmother smelled like a lack of sex. Even her kitchen was dry, the cans of bargain vegetables, the rice cooked too long. The toast without butter under the jam. I starved there. Not for lack of calories but from an internal thirst for moistness, for acknowledgement of my new breasts, my dark-red-stained underpants soaking in her sink, for the promise from somewhere that my femaleness would not be wasted on me, shamed out of me, or denied by me. I vow, under my breath, under her covers I will find someone to touch me or even touch myself. I will learn to move my hips, serve butter melting on warm brown bread with honey, and cocoa made with cream. I will wear red lipstick and slips and sheer everything. I will wet-kiss my grandchildren, let myself cry at my son's funeral, cling to my rights, believe in my own juices. I pray my grandmother will die soon, before I see who is on the inside, before I internalize her cracked elbows, knees, lips, and feet. Before she tells me what happened to her throbbing heart.

II

Grandpa took his music underground to the red-walled, red-floored basement, played along to scratchy jazz records, big bands with glitzy names glittered on cardboard music stands, a woman named Mahalia, who my grandmother suspected he was thinking of when he was sleeping with her. Under flannel night covers, Grandpa yearned for black satin skin, and an on-pitch moan at just the right time. The grandchildren gathered around the bass drum, reached for the microphone, banged xylophone mallets together more than on the keys. Grandpa played to us, sang to us. Finally an audience, applause, laughter, dancers. Upstairs Grandma cooked and worried over suggestive lyrics, the red clay stains, the hearing loss. She never sang, not even in church, or in the car alone to stay awake. No music lessons for her, only how to milk, calf, call the men to supper, unsaddle, comb, wash, and dry. Fine lessons, even important, but of no use when her whole heart and aching chest want to join in song, strike a chord, kick her guilt-ridden heels upwards toward heaven, toward the singing, dancing angels of love.

III

Maybe this is my grandmother, the green eyes and the daisies strung in her hair, my own dimples, crooked eye teeth and early greying hair. She is serious. She knows too well that the world is violent, uncaring, full of winter. She calls herself Momo, lover of plants and dogs and once a man. He was not my grandfather. Her whimsy has fooled many, fooled herself on occasion when life was too easily about the next moving picture to move through town, about who married whom and used to live on the corner. And why is train travel suddenly only for the orphaned, widowed old? When she looks too long in the mirror and forgets to stop gardening in the rain, she finds herself and knows the universe, all that her past, all that never will and most of what's to come. She knows her own rhythms are the earth's, her memories are not her own, that desires do not lessen with age but rename themselves rage and triumph, becoming near-death experiences. I see her walking now, her legs hidden by skirt and swaying grasses, her feet bare, hips full. She is not moving toward me. I do not call her home to my house where she might find forgetfulness in the daily soaps, the guest room, my children's bath time. I watch her move. She is searching her own solitude and grief, remembering her humor, her whimsy, her throaty laughter, moist eyes. I believe she works for justice and change, a less hostile world for my son's daughters and grandsons. I know her life has lived beyond assigned roles, committee work and relationships of obligations. I hope she is leaving tracks, patting the grasses down, dropping corn or locks of grey, leaving me a train I might follow through my own mirror, across a muddy garden, and home.

IV

You call yourself childless. Still, I call myself your grandbaby, recognize your arms, breasts, soft thumbs, calloused palms, nurse's watch, your married to Jesus ring, silver and red, a circle of crosses. We make a circle of two. Hot water for tea between us. And fifty years, a continent, and respectful, generous, bountiful love. You have cared for soldiers, recently separated from loved ones, limbs, and hope. I cradle your head, close your eyes on nightmares, this November cold snap, the late night news of conflict, bombs in small foreign lands. The third world sneaks up behind us, threatening competition, equality, violence, more of ourselves. Fear is real and deserved. You know France is not full of romantic Paris nights but of graves, teenaged ghosts, your undiscovered past and unrecovered future. Still tonight you and I are at least at peace. We rock to the midnight big band hour as you move back in memory time. Some of our children are dead, some we only imagine are safe.

V

Call me granddaughter please, just once. My hair is your own. I too collect earrings, colored swede, bags to hold books and chocolate recipes. I am of you, your bent back, heavy hands, no rings around your soft knuckles as you squeeze my broad shoulders, a greeting between two women, one waltzing with middle age, one nearing ninety years of knowing. Knowing the singing and shouting that I have longed these forty-five years to hear—"go forth, step firmly, trust the earth under you, the stars overhead and those who have left a trail for you. These few have won and lost their fear so that you might walk through walls without doorways, without the secret handshake. So that you might travel recklessly over disbelievers, their packed trunks of doubt, despair, and empty notebooks. So that you might write, garden, and dance in the knowing light of peaceful significance."

VI

I believe you are my grandmother. Your hair straight, grey, short. Your black crepe cape brushes me as you move, softly, surely in suede heels, front to back of the room filled with women, younger than you wanting to be near you as you bite down hard on patriarchal academia, the female impersonators we, too, often impersonate, behind painted lips, well-defined brows, and strained smiles. We are your children, your daughters. But we have not met, have not imagined that your life is real, a possibility for woman, for me, for my sisters, mother, and suckling daughter. I want to know what you eat for breakfast, if you sleep with a man, have you endured childbirth, midnight feedings, the scorn of a mother-in-law, a jealous father, the redemption of spirit through sweat and laughter and the moon overhead? You promise light on the path, a universe of nearness and head thrown back in laughter. Steel blue eyes meet mine, a clear voice piercing my ears. "Read Audre Lorde, read *The Cancer Journals*, read Adrienne Rich, read *On Lies, Secrets, and Silence*." The path you promise is rich and flowered with blood and thunder. I swallow these gifts, step forward. Open my palms. I serve you as we move into a new century where girl babies will look to the river for food and to our eyes for the fullness of hope, for the fruit the texture of possibility. As mouths close over our separateness, we merge, expand and become dark real power, pure scarlet hope between my future granddaughter's legs.

Big Sale Today

No one times the disposable
Diapers right or the formula
Or the baby wipes. Always
Half packages remain.

Every mother's lap empties out.
Still mine did so in a second,
In the space that should have
Divided one breath from the next.

Become silence forever.
Today, beside two car seats, one crib,
Three boxes of board books,
One stroller, one swing set,

Pooh Bear, Tigger, and Owl.
Unopened Play-Doh jars,
Three-bedroom house and van,
All the unsung nursery rhymes,

And dreams of Little League wins,
I long to put my body—
Arms, hips and singing lungs—
On my garage sale today.

In the yard and for sale now, cheap.
But no one wants to buy from us.
Might be selling dark luck.
I change the sign by noon.

Dead child's toys for free, help yourself.
I go back into my vacant house
Then back out, add in bold
Cancer is not catching.

Unmothering

I

Shortened contracts. Finished before you know it. Time flies. Mothering time at quantum speed. My own mother so resigned to her death at fifty-two I have to invent pictures of her fighting for her life, fighting for the chance to keep mothering me. To see my children, to listen to my breast feeding and first day of school dramas. If she thought of this she never mentioned it to me, or to my sisters, who lost her even sooner than I did. One before the high school graduation walking-across-the-stage blurry picture could be taken. Did my mother apologize to her? I would feel like a better person if I were mad at cancer instead of furious at her. Lovely and thin at last in her final weeks, and finally filling her closet with the size sixes she had so long longed for, lived for, now was willing to die for if someone would assure her she didn't look fat in anything anymore.

She became friendly with death, waited not wholly patiently as she planned her funeral songs and readings. Something not too Catholic or sad, the two being inseparable to her by then. To be Catholic is to be filled with the darkness of two Marys and lines of lonely men in drag, wishing for love, hating the men who came to them for blessed wafer and wine, men who longed and loved in the acceptable ways, no need to hide, to cry into the foam of borrowed pillows at night.

It would be a Catholic funeral, but someone would read Alice Walker too and Elie Wiesel and Pablo Neruda. Such richness one might think that life was worth sticking around for. But my mother dove into dying like she had never opened to life. Like a dull novel that finally grips you in the final chapter and makes you glad for going on, hanging in there instead of walking to the drug store in the dark for something grittier, deeper, more beautiful.

I was twenty-four, unhappily married, underemployed, my whole life ahead of me and eager enough to get to it, to get through her death to the rest of my life. Unaware in the blissful way of young adulthood, wrapped in the safety of smooth skin and strong, straight legs, that other abortions were to come, unbidden and certain as tulips in a Midwest grey-brown Spring.

II

Ten years later, I pushed my second son into the world, sweating, but peaceful in the bargain: this pain for the close-up view of his life, a near-certain mourner at my own funeral someday. Someone to join his brother in the private terrain of siblinghood, rolling eyes and meaningful looks across the hundreds of holiday tables to come. In my birthing pain, I assumed the rolling decades ahead, assumed the inevitable adoration, disgust, respect, pity, attachment and grief. Assumed my own right to the expected so hard I forgot to pray for it.

Healthy children. It's how my sisters and I consoled ourselves, both our parents dead before their social security could kick in. But we had such beautiful, smart children. Surely this next generation was our reward for loss so well lived, no sojourns into self-pity allowed, gratitude like a too-big vitamin pill we all swallowed with breakfast, scraping our throats all the way down. Some days it stuck somewhere, in the way of all we would try to nourish ourselves with or sing later. Still nothing stops time and its losses. Time like an anxious lover, always on its way to the sunset and back again to rise without him, without her. At thirty-nine, I'm again left to consider what remains and what's still possible. These the real questions of grief. Not why once again years of mothering would be denied, scraped from the soft red tissue surrounding my beating heart and flung nowhere.

Only Child

Suddenly, my surviving son turns twelve, nearly a teenager, stretching to be taller than me, his face newly oily, his hair in his eyes and he likes it as much as I hate it. He is double the age he was when his brother died. When I ask him if he remembers the yellow and blue play room shaped like a pirate ship at the university hospital or the way his brother used to ask for suckers in the middle of the night he looks at me blankly and says I don't remember anything and don't ask me again. But I do. I want him to share my memories. I want to be less alone. I want him to miss him. When we travel in a nearby but foreign country we get a single bed by mistake. And he says, "I'll sleep on the floor, like Kevin did." And when I say, "What?" just to hear it again, just to hear him say his dead brother's name because I long to hear it in my house, in my car, all the places I expected to be calling out to him, stop it Kevin, get in here Kevin, I mean it Kevin Steven. But he won't repeat it, only rolls his eyes at me, stares at the city street so many stories below us, where tomorrow we'll walk around and sample vendor food and drink too much coffee and pretend that he is an only child.

What Remains

Some things remained. I still found comfort in the voices of Bonnie Raitt and Van Morrison and KD Lang. I still sang along, off key and unconcerned. I still wrote three pages each day in spiral bound notebooks. Ramblings, sometimes interesting sometimes as mundane as yesterday's coffee, cold and familiar, unsurprising and therefore good. I still wandered the halls at night with groggy residents and housekeeping staff, drunk family members summoned here in the middle of the night, unlike me, too stunned to find belonging, all of us too scared to sit still. I still drank too much coffee and I read fiction by contemporary American women and because my children were young I still watched public television and Cartoon Network. No hard news. Sometimes in the middle of the night, I watched hurricane reports from a thousand miles away and felt safe.

Mothers United

I went to college in the seventies, which among other things means that most of my friends had at least one abortion. I didn't. It was legal by then, though we had to drive five hours to Minneapolis. The adoption agency was just across from city hall. Some of those friends had children later, sparklingly highly intelligent children to brag about at our twenty year reunion. Some didn't, some couldn't, took drugs and their own temperature for years, bled long after they'd given up god and his promises of forgiveness. Some of those sparkling children drove snowmobiles and motorcycles into culverts and some disappeared into a cloud of student loans and pot smoke, dead as my son, but walking around somewhere. Some took on stepchildren who refused to call them mom and husbands who cried through holidays. By our thirty year reunion, I wasn't the only one who didn't know how to answer the benign question: Do you have kids? Some still dream of a call from an adoption agency. Someone looking for them after all these years. Some still have nightmares of blood and mucus running for days without a name. Some still hope for grandchildren, another glance at goodness in the eyes of a human animal. All of us have broken hearts in the form of a child's fist, pudgy, full of promise.

Gravy, High Heels

Someday you'll be dead
For a long time.
My grandmother says this
Stirring gravy
In baby blue high heels and nude hose
Without concern or reverence
And when I tell this small slice of
Her story, of her saying this to me
When I am ten or twelve or fifteen
Years old,
When she thought I was
Too scared, too sad, too unwound,
Friends gasp and laugh
Like all good stories
It is alive and therefore evolving
Sometimes her heels are candy apple red
Or bedroom slippers with feathers.
Sometimes I am angry and sometimes
I am too thrilled by some teenaged
Opportunity or a boy who
Doesn't like me back.
Forty years away from her
Roast beef and scalloped corn
Sunday dinner table,
Her at one end, grandpa smoking
Pall Malls at the other,
I know she was telling me of love
With all its edges and risk and
Simple beauty.
Of wishing for more
And holding too tight
Of learning to sit beside
Without commentary or surprise

Of learning to love every moment
Just coming after the last
Even though the gravy is never prefect
It's way too alive
And like my heart will never
Be still and predictable.

Mess

It's a city. It's a mess.
We are a family.
We don't share one
Memory.
Except this:
Everyone died too young.
At fifty-two
At sixty-three
At ninety-four.
Goddamn, she almost
Made it to ninety-five.
Unfinished lives
Everywhere,
Unsure with no
Conclusion, spinning
Earth like, in trust
That every wave reaches
Somewhere
And anywhere is as
Good as anywhere else.

So I get up earlier
Than I need to and write
Poetry and go to sleep
On poetry that I refuse
To capture, write down.
Surely a sin on my part,
But I will not begin
The morning with no,
Rather yes to the verse
In my head
Coming awake barely aware
Is it raining or sunny?

Are you here with me?
Disembodied lines
No bitter food image yet attached
To awaken in my reader
His mouth, her heart
Some urge to live longer
Some desire to reach out
Like all decent verse will
Do. Tidy up a world.

The Worst Loss

I didn't have to look far to find other mothers who had buried their children, my grandmother, the mother of my best friend, my other grandmother's mother, my husband's grandmother, and a circle of us monthly at Compassionate Friends meetings, a church basement, Kleenex boxes, similar stories, no urging to move on here. The worst loss became a cliché I refused to believe in. The very specialness of it an insult to my grandmother and all the rest. Too safe, too rare and a lie. Dying children are as common as the prairie wells that women threw themselves down commonly, tragically, no less harsh and pitiful because it happened all the time. Just another thing we don't talk about. Only here in the Sunday night circle of parents, we don't feel out of sync with the cycle of nature because we're still breathing, working, eating, working out, loving, even laughing. Over and over, we tell how it happened, slowly in a hospital bed or suddenly under the ski of a snowmobile. Something so unavoidable, something so wrong. And so common. Children who are only human and therefore fragile and sometimes weightless when they sleep. I have the same sense of being cheated as when my milk came in with a searing pain. No one told me. Like sorority hazing secrets. Her son killed on his bike at a railroad crossing, her a motorcycle accident, her leukemia, her heart trouble from birth, me cancer. We meet each other's eyes because no one else will. Together we chant the one thing that might save us if brownies and decaffeinated coffee won't. Children die first sometimes. It happens, it always has and it always will.

Evidence

I wasn't cleaning or even organizing. More like what my mother would have called putzing, when a pile of rainbow-colored shirts came raining down on me, and amongst them, a square of pink tissue paper that landed on my bare left foot. As the cotton shapes unfolded themselves, names of summer camps, vacation destinations and tee-ball teams spread poem-like on the floor. Mackinac Island, Paul Bunyan Land, Deer Town, Mount Rushmore, Bayview Tigers, City Center Rascals, Disneyland, USA. The tissue paper was less familiar. I touched it, opened the folded pink, so like a child's mouth, to three tiny teeth. Kevin's teeth of course, when his body was still doing the usual things I wanted it to do: discard baby teeth, grow hair, run bases, land in mom and dad's bed during thunderstorms. Before the black cancer cells grew faster than the doctors could come up with a new plan to kill them without killing him. I lifted the white jagged evidence that I had once been a mother of two, dropped them one by one on my tongue, closed my mouth and sucked hard.

Counting

This place doesn't have the charm of a 1950s American diner, but it's as close as the 1970s could get. There is a phone in every booth to call our order of cheese frenchies for everyone, deep fried grilled cheese sandwiches, and onion rings for two and fries for three, and chocolate shakes all around, not malts, my sister is allergic. All through the crunchy meal, my mother is bent over a thin piece of typing paper, a pink Tab can at her elbow, writing in her curvy, careful printing, words we can't see but long to read. It's her Christmas shopping list. A complicated grid to balance six children, a railroad man's salary, her deep need not to show favoritism. Even as I sink my teeth through the crisp outside to the greasy middle layer of white bread to the hot, melted orange cheese, I hope this Saturday afternoon treat won't count too much against us come Christmas morning. We are too old to stack and count each sister's pile of brightly wrapped presents, but we will anyway, just to pass the time. Besides it makes her efforts to make it all even seem worthwhile. I pretend to not like the burnt French Fries at the bottom of my basket, and mom eats them so they won't go to waste and because they are her favorite and all she'll have for lunch. My mother is always on a diet, though I don't see anything happening. Her body is soft and round, and I mistake her tight clothes for a need to buy a bigger size not a need to make her body smaller. She assures me that I will understand one day that if she bought a different size she would just let herself grow into it, and I realize that the rules for mom clothes must be very different than for kid clothes. We all grow out of our clothes by the end of the school year and it seems to be a good thing. That isn't all that separated us but it did make a difference.

II

I walked around for months after my baby died saying to anyone who would listen what am I going to do now? Mostly my sisters were listening because everyone else was afraid of me, so much bad luck on my breath, after months of walking the halls of cancer wards, pushing my two-year-old son in his wheel chair that he called his fancy chair, decorated as it was with Tigger and Winnie the Pooh balloons and Teletubbies stickers. On a good day we would both smile at other bald children, who sometimes had the strength to lift their heads and smile back. But too often their eyes were closed and a mom or dad would pretend to lift the corners of their own mouths and say her counts are really down today, we're just waiting for some platelets to get up here. And I would say take care and act like that was a perfectly reasonable thing to be doing. Waiting for plastic bags of blood to arrive so our children would look like they were alive as they waited more patiently than their stunned parents for more bad news, a worse prognosis, or the harshly hopeful news that a new drug was being tested in Texas and so far not killing all the subjects in the trial.

III

After we buried him in his Gap jeans, Old Navy tee shirt, and batman socks, I kept walking, now on city streets and the circled paths through the cemetery across the street from my two-story house. In the Fall, I can see his gravestone through the bare lilac bushes from my front porch, a heart-shaped black marble stone, the corniest thing I've ever done. My mother-in-law plants another bleeding heart every spring, next to his name, the dates, so somehow it all comes together I suppose. I had long since stopped expecting an answer when my sister says write about it already. Like it's the most obvious thing in the world for a writer who is also a mother. But it's not that simple, because I have another son and what if he ever stacks the poems and essays up and counts? I have no grid. I buy my clothes too big so I can feel the fabric move and my breath can be full. I will never trust myself to be fair.

Icy Roads

You match your stride to mine, grab my hand in both of yours, lace your fingers over mine. I pull away. You hold on. I start laughing because that's what I do when I'm nervous, when I'm angry, when I'm nervously angry, when I am that girl not allowed mad or silly or loud feelings of any color. I laugh as you tug at my elbow and I pull harder in the other direction, toward my soft belly. My hand snaps out of your grip. "Oh," you say, "was your backpack falling?" It couldn't, secure and buckled twice over my chest. Still, I say, "Yes, I needed my hand." It's a lie. Lying is a verb and laughing is a lie in this story. I pull away because I want to be free. I know how to lose things, not how to hold on. Would I be this mean without my too-big helping of grief? My hand finds my pocket, makes a tight fist. It's icy and I slip a little, walk faster, with shorter steps. My legs are longer than yours and I know this. You struggle to keep up. I pretend to reach for you when you nearly fall. But really I make sure my hand does not touch your sleeve.

Defiant Gardeners

Long napping under the warm quilt of grief
Broken hearted mid-life oasis
Bitter chocolate, dry red wine
Sweetened oolong tea. Unsalted butter
Hard cheese, deep sweaty yoga.
Coming back to the world so loved.

Interior rhymes and folk art
Even yard art, Saint Teresa, Mother Mary
Wailing walls where love lies bleeding
Blooming too late into fall.

Conceptual us in the back row
Of this gallery talk
Artists, philosophers, architects,
Gardeners all wondering together
Why this simple act of growing green things
Makes such a different life.

And me wondering
Where you are, why I didn't see you earlier
At the candidate's fundraiser and last week
At the acoustic festival
All gardens representing the first
Apples and snakes everywhere and alike.

Add naked man, naked woman
The energy of the Buddha's triad and
Crane Island. Mountain to the north.
Water exiting to the southwest
Heat of moving on, waking finally
That quilt too warm, damp, and heavy.

When the windows blow open I know
The path knows my name again.

Compatriots: Columbine and Red Lake

I'm reading a book called *We Need To Talk About Kevin*, really though I could barely buy it without choking, and I hide it from my husband and son because it's not about our Kevin, gone now for longer than he was here. Kevin of the novel is a teenaged school shooting gunman. But I don't read it for him, or to understand him. I read it greedily, like a starved carnivore, for his mother, who, of course, is fictional too, like this violent Kevin. Still I am drawn to her, like an addict to sugar, alcohol, the shopping channel, desperate, guilty. Another mother destroyed by a son, falling off a cliff, in her hand the ticket to Paris we all buy with the home pregnancy test that somehow lands us in Holland. A life of trying to love tulips. My own craving for croissants and espresso, long ago placed on the altar of early middle age; I sink into her soft interior cocktail, despair sweetened by disbelief. I couldn't keep my son alive and she couldn't keep her son from killing twelve other children with mothers. She is my compatriot now. I am her only hope for empathy, an understanding, a love, miles past false forgiveness or too quick new age acceptance. Company in the dark human heart where children die before their mothers and their mothers hate them for it.

Second Born

It's only a theory, and that's all it will ever be. I sometimes find it comforting, and I sometimes find it terrifying. Sometimes I don't much care either way. I was the second born, same sex as the first born so a disappointment to a couple of generations, waiting patiently for my dark arrival. My older sister was by then a beauty by all northern European standards. Blonde, fair, blue eyes, naturally full of Midwestern self-doubt and charm. Girly. I arrived with straight black hair and my father's mean eyes, focused already on my sister's every weakness, most notably her resemblance to my mother. Of course I was innocent as all babies are, empty, not holy, but lovely all the same. My mother loved me when she wasn't too busy flirting with my father or curling my sister's long silky hair. My own hair grew in tufts, none over a few inches for the first five years of my life. Arguably ugly or at least pitiful. My likeness to my father brought to me his self-loathing finally externalized. He offered me disdain and I didn't know how to refuse him or that I could, so I couldn't. On my best days I felt invisible. Unseen, unhurt, and peaceful. My mother's death at an early age was sad but I didn't miss her. I had never had her. But then maybe I did ten years later. Maybe she came to me, reincarnated as my second-born child, my second son, unbidden, and unexpected, loved and celebrated like an extra full moon or a comet, an easy baby by all measure, beautiful as a Swedish prince, so like his auntie, fair and blonde and cheerful. His body slid out of me with ease. He teethed painlessly, crawled and walked and talked early. None of his brother's stubbornness, or his father's ruddy complexion or my fierce and choice-less emotion. Mothers love their children, unearned and perfectly. Even me, her second born, thoughtlessly, surely, completely.

The Hairpiece

When my friend Cindy, teacher of the mystical tarot, was dying, we brushed her hair into our circle of twenty four hands and spread it grey and glistening onto her lilac bushes along the frozen Red River. She refused hard copies of all the get well e-mail arriving because her need to read them was so little next to the trees it would cost us all to print them. A month earlier, resting in her camper with her oxygen tank, and all of us near, by the campfire with wine, olives, and strong cheese, she expends some of the last of her Amazon strength to warn us that we are confusing modernism with post-modernism.

I told both these stories at her Catholic-style Unitarian Universalism wake and everyone laughed in recognition—the best of us found in the center of her. I started growing my hair the next day. It grew fast as it always had, a reminder of something unchanged. Like Mary Oliver poetry at weddings and funerals, everything in between. I felt different right away. After decades of appointments every three weeks religious as the yearly fights with my husband about the total at the bottom of the hair column in our budget, I felt both more and less like myself, full.

I could feel it on my head when I danced and in my face when I made love and soon on my neck so I could give up my itchy wool scarf except on the coldest days, double digits below zero and wind. She wanted the birds to make nests and comfort of it. I wanted someone to notice its wave and volume. Like an old friend who shouted across a crowded coffee shop, holy long hair, my seventh-grade self seen at last.

They think it's just hair my husband told me, not a sacred symbol of what's still possible. They don't know about hair like you do. Like someone who has lifted it by handful from my son's head where it lay, unattached, disenfranchised as me, someone who stuffed an ice cap so my mother's graying curls might survive chemo therapy even if she didn't, someone who watched her own texture change childhood surgery to childhood surgery, straight and oily to dry frizz to soft curl. Just a reaction to different anesthesia they told my perplexed mother. Still, how could she know who this daughter was when her hair kept changing?

So I cut it off and kept cutting it until I too needed to know who I was. Wavy unless coaxed hard. Neither blond nor brown or gray just yet. Here in the middle of my life to the middle of my back between my shoulder blades. Put up, pulled back, let go, straightened. Choice, like a white elephant, ought to be good for something someday.

Maybe the birds came but maybe it was already too deep into winter. Maybe some strands survived until the desperate spring migration and are famous now as in the year of the softest nest ever. Maybe those chicks never wanted to leave such a beautiful home and maybe those chicks grew to be birds of a nature stronger and surer of surprises and beauty. Maybe the songs I hear out my door are those birds, surely grandmothers by now, noticing my hair, coveting it for a next generation of their own.

Later in Nashville

Summer 2005 was an American hurricane nightmare. I was in Nashville for a conference, music city, loud and in tune despite the despair to the south, its own borders expanding as Rita threatened to follow Katrina, like a meaner but smaller little sister. Downtown, music all day, live and rhythmic, made by bartenders and nannies by night. We were all falling in love with the lead singer, and she was just rough enough to make us ache and soft enough to meet our eyes as she passed the tip jar during a drum solo, too long, but for this purpose, necessary. I made a bathroom trip and found a fan from the table behind me weeping, in a squat, knees bent, elbows between, head in spread fingers, in a position that most of the world's women cook in but here in the USA is oddly awkward outside a yoga class. I asked her if she was okay, if she needed her sister, who I know is back at the table singing along to Merle Haggard, swaying sweetly, gin, neat with a twist of lime. My sister had been half at their table and half at mine most of the night. They smoke; I don't so the bond was instant and drug-like. I felt a little left out and maybe that made me join her, limber from years of palates and a little drunk myself. She leaned into me and we both fell butt down on the cement floor, her head on my shoulder, my hand on her forehead to steady us both. I know this is silly she says, it's a great night, you and your sister are the best and my mother has the kids and this town is a lot like home. But we lost everything. I miss my tea kettle and my lavender down comforter and I wonder if the jewelry store that we owe big time for this ring lost its records and I don't know how to laugh and cry at the same time but I'm learning. We both know it's the way on from here. Let me tell you about Kevin, and then I want to hear more about your house. Was it shotgun, antebellum, or a twin home? Did you have a nice yard in New Orleans?

The Reading Cure

I took to reading like other grieving mothers might take to Darvoset or chocolate chip cookie dough ice cream or *Dynasty* reruns. We all seek the deep stillness and empty eyes of a peaceful and unmessy Houdini act. From the sublime and elegant *The Disappearance* by Genevieve Jurgensen to the naïve comfort of *The Worst Loss* by Barbara D. Rosof and the absurd *Quit Kissing My Ashes* by Judy Collier. Not the sweet suspense of Agatha or Deepak's transcendentalism. But the voices of my lonely invisible peers. Other women who have followed a small casket into a crowded, high-ceilinged room. Other women who have seen the blood pressure go away just before the in breath is never released ever. Other women running from the unspeakable failure to keep their own children alive. And they wrote it.

Time Clock Cure

Most people thought I went back to work too soon. Not that they told me, of course they were way too scared of me to be that honest. They just raised their eyebrows or said really, already or are you sure or why so soon. And I said what else am I supposed to do, it's what I do it's my trade, my skill. Not unlike a factory worker, really, not unlike you. So I went back and not once did I utter after another should I leave or should I stay song, who cares, my baby died. Never did I scream it at a middle aged, middle class client sobbing into my box of Kleenex because not once did his mother, forty years ago and strapped with nine other kids, come to see him play basketball. And he was really good. It might be the only thing he has ever been good at. In response to stories of swearing teenagers and demanding aging parents, I was quiet and unconcerned, empathic and articulate. Because the lesson of dying is living until you do. And the angels know nothing about too soon or too late and all time is unraveled in heaven, a soft landing for us all.

Unwatched

In an old doctor's medical bookcase with its lifting glass and small brass buttons, under my dead mother's books and my own mostly unread poetry volumes—bought at readings that made me weep and later I can't imagine why. There on the floor shelf, two VHS black rectangle dusty plastic cases. Soon we won't own a machine capable of playing them to life and I will be relieved. I will be technologically unable to see my niece Justine reading a sweet and rhyming poem and her dad, my sister's then-husband straining to hit the notes of a sad country western song about a boy who I can't figure out if died or just grew up and his mother in her middle-class solipsism mourns his empty room and the lack of smelly laundry between Labor Day and Thanksgiving. I won't be able to see my own straight back as I follow my six-year-old son into the front pew. I won't possibly be able to hear the sermon offered up in honor of a child too young to have earned anything so serious and literate, or my husband, muffled noises coming from his face, buried in his red hands. And most importantly, I won't be able to see my father's look of disdain on my own face when I look across my son's blond head to his father.

Condolences

People say all kinds of crazy things, stupid things, thoughtless things, mostly things no one will remember anyway, like the funeral sermon. Things like crying helps or time heals and I couldn't do it. As if god shows you the card and asks if you'd like to pass or take it, discard or play it. As if god pays attention to the pot full of rosary and prayer chain requests pulls it to himself and pays out in miracles, clean MRIs and low tumor counts. As if god is a he and we can possibly imagine one thing about divinity with our human minds. As if someone is in charge. But I can have my fantasies. A god who would throw lightning into the aisles of St. Leo's Catholic Church, strike dead a blue-haired, stooped woman who says to me as she grabs me by the elbow and leads me away from my second born's coffin, his tattered Pooh blanket and retinaless eyes, At least you'll never lose him to another woman. That's what usually happens you know.

Sunday Driving

I'm feeling better
I'm getting closer
You are driving through town
A trailer full of horses
You could stop by
It was so good to talk
No that didn't mean that
But I'm feeling better
I'm getting closer.

You are sorry that you want
So much from me
You want to be different
Than you are, but
There was that childhood
And all the confusion.
No it will not work for me
But I'm feeling better
I'm getting closer.

My father died
My mother died
I do not cry when your dog dies
It's no excuse

My baby died, my grandma lived too long
I understand nothing
But I'm getting better
I'm feeling closer
To someone who I barely know
I crave the dark
You crave attention
I scare you

You call me crazy
The blinds are closed
The roads are blocked
The blizzard is worse than anyone
Could have guessed
But I'm getting closer
I'm feeling better
All the while.
You sell your house
I buy my peace of mind

We don't know who
Is supposed to lead
No slow dancing
Only solo camping
Invitations from the lonely
Still I'm getting closer
And I'm feeling better
Now that you're gone.

Acknowledgments

I'm most grateful to all my teachers all these years, especially Margaret Woell, Bonniejean Christensen, Mark Vinz, and Karla Smart-Morstad.

I am forever thankful for the immeasurerable support and faith in my written words from Cathy Williams, Tim Johnson, Ev Rerick, Vi Ratchenski, Emma Jahnke, Justine Winterowd, Cali Anicha, Laurie Baker, Kevin Zepper, and Carrie Carter.

So many people carried me, including Joe Kapaun, Susy Lemar, Mary Kay Boeshans, Kathy Papietro, Deb Chambers, Susie Ekberg Risher, Trish Strom, Leslie Sinner McEvoy, Brooke Waslien Fradet, Brianne Waslien Stoffel and the hundreds of nurses who cared for us all.

Finally my heart will always hold Dr. Patrick Welle, Dr. Corey Raffel and Dr. Nathan Kobrinsky, who when couldn't cure, loved instead.

The following selections have been previously published in some form:

Sailor Mom, Sing Along, and Evidence: *Dust & Fire: Writing & Art by Women*, 20th Anniversary Edition, An Anthology, Volume XX, March 2006. Women Studies, Bemidji State University, Bemidji, Minnesota.

Big Sale Today: *The Cancer Poetry Project: Poems by Cancer Patients and Those Who Love Them*, An Anthology edited by Karen B. Miller, Fairview Press, Minneapolis, Minnesota, 2001.

Gravy, High Heels, and Icy Roads: *Red Weather,* Issue Number 33, Spring 2014, poetry, prose, visual art, Minnesota State University Moorhead, Moorhead, Minnesota.

About the Author

Carol Kapaun Ratchenski began writing prose poetry in the 80s after reading *Murder in the Dark* by Margaret Atwood. *The House on the Mango Street* by Sandra Cisneros took her breath away. Ratchenski's first novel, *Mamababy*, was published in 2013 as an e-book by Knuckledown Press. Years after losing her second born son to cancer in 1999, she decided to write about it and about all the ways that life is horrible and wonderful all at the same time, and how that is something beautiful.

Kapaun Ratchenski's work has also appeared in *Gypsy Cab*, *Red Weather*, *North Dakota Quarterly*, *Wintercount*, *Lake Region Review*, *Dust and Fire*, *NDSU Magazine*, and the anthologies *Resurrecting Grace: Remembering Catholic Childhoods*, edited by Marilyn Sewell, Beacon Press, 2001, and *The Cancer Poetry Project: Poems by Cancer Patients and Those Who Love Them*, edited by Karen B. Miller, Fairview Press, 2001.

She has been a Licensed Professional Counselor in North Dakota since 1993 and is owner/operator of Center for Compassion and Creativity in Fargo, ND, where she also lives.

About New Rivers Press

New Rivers Press emerged from a drafty Massachusetts barn in winter 1968. Intent on publishing work by new and emerging poets, founder C. W. "Bill" Truesdale labored for weeks over an old Chandler & Price letterpress to publish three hundred fifty copies of Margaret Randall's collection, So Many Rooms Has a House But One Roof.

Nearly four hundred titles later, New Rivers, a non-profit and now teaching press based since 2001 at Minnesota State University Moorhead, has remained true to Bill's goal of publishing the best new literature—poetry and prose—from new, emerging, and established writers.

New Rivers Press authors range in age from twenty to eighty-nine. They include a silversmith, a carpenter, a geneticist, a monk, a tree-trimmer, and a rock musician. They hail from cities such as Christchurch, Honolulu, New Orleans, New York City, Northfield (Minnesota), and Prague.

Charles Baxter, one of the first authors with New Rivers, calls the press "the hidden backbone of the American literary tradition." Continuing this tradition, in 1981 New Rivers began to sponsor the Minnesota Voices Project (now called Many Voices Project) competition. It is one of the oldest literary competitions in the United States, bringing recognition and attention to emerging writers. Other New Rivers publications include the American Fiction Series, the American Poetry Series, New Rivers Abroad, and the Electronic Book Series.

Please visit our website **newriverspress.com** for more information.

Many Voices Project Award Winners

("OP" indicates that the paper copy is out of print; "e-book" indicates that the title is available as an electronic publication.)

#134 It Turns Out Like This, Stephen Coyne (e-book)
#133 A Beautiful Hell, Carol Kapaun Ratchenski
#132 Home Studies, Julie Gard (e-book)
#131 Flashcards & The Curse of Ambrosia, Tracy Robert (e-book)
#130 Dispensations, Randolph Thomas (e-book)
#129 Invasives, Brandon Krieg
#128 Whitney, Joe Stracci (e-book)
#127 Rare Earth, Bradford Tice
#126 The Way of All Flux, Sharon Suzuki-Martinez
#125 It Takes You Over, Nick Healy (e-book)
#124 The Muse of Ocean Parkway and Other Stories, Jacob Lampart (e-book)
#123 Hotel Utopia, Robert Miltner
#122 Kinesthesia, Stephanie N. Johnson
#121 Birds of Wisconsin, B.J. Best
#120 At Home Anywhere, Mary Hoffman (e-book)
#119 Friend Among Stones, Maya Pindyck
#118 Fallibility, Elizabeth Oness
#117 When Love Was Clean Underwear, Susan Barr-Toman (e-book)
#116 The Sound of It, Tim Nolan
#115 Hollow Out, Kelsea Habecker
#114 Bend from the Knees, Benjamin Drevlow
#113 The Tender, Wild Things, Diane Jarvenpa
#112 Signaling for Rescue, Marianne Herrmann
#111 Cars Go Fast, John Chattin
#110 Terrain Tracks, Purvi Shah
#109 Numerology and Other Stories, Christian Michener
#108 Not a Matter of Love, Beth Alvarado (e-book)
#107 Real Karaoke People, Ed Bok Lee

#106 Love in An Expanding Universe, Ron Rindo
#105 Second Language, Ronna Wineberg (e-book)
#104 Landing Zones, Edward Micus
#103 The Volunteer, Candace Black
#102 Nice Girls and Other Stories, Cezarija Abartis
#101 Paper Boat, Cullen Bailey Burns
#99 Mozart's Carriage, Daniel Bachhuber
#98 The Pact, Walter Roers
#97 Alone with the Owl, Alan Davis
#96 Rafting on the Water Table, Susan Steger Welsh
#95 Woman Lake, Richard Broderick
#94 The Record Player and Other Stories, Winifred Moranville
#93 Casting Lines, Orval Lund
#92 Dakota Incarnate: A Collection of Short Stories, Bill McDonald
#91 Vendettas, Charms, and Prayers, Pamela Gemin
#90 An Alchemy in the Bones, William Reichard
#89 Music of the Inner Lakes, Roger Sheffer
#88 The Fragile Peace You Keep, Kel Munger
#87 The Dirty Shame Hotel and Other Stories, Ron Block
#85 Sermon on a Perfect Spring Day, Philip Bryant (e-book)
#84 Rootbound, Jeanne Emmons
#83 Bonfire, Connie Wanek
#82 Laundromat Blues, Lupe Solis
#81 The Natural Father, Robert Lacy
#80 Self Storage, Mary Helen Stefaniak
#79 Fishing for Myth, Heid E. Erdrich
#78 Sustenance, Aaron Anstett
#77 On the Road to Patsy Cline, John Reinhard
#76 Remembering China 1935-1945, Bea Exner Liu
#75 The Dance Hall at Spring Hill, Duke Klassen (e-book)
#74 Divining the Landscape, Diane Jarvenpa
#73 To Collect the Flesh, Greg Hewett

#72 Heathens, David Haynes

#71 Secrets Men Keep, Ron Rindo

#70 Everything's a Verb, Debra Marquart

#69 Revealing the Unknown to a Pair of Lovers, Ann Lundberg Grunke

#68 What They Always Were, Norita Dittberner-Jax

#67 Coming Up for Light and Air, Barbara Crow

#66 Mal D'Afrique, Jarda Cervenka (e-book)

#65 Aerial Studies, Sandra Adelmund Witt

#64 The Peace Terrorist, Carol Masters

#63 Thin Ice and Other Risks, Gary Eller

#62 Falling in Love at the End of the World, Rick Christman

#61 This House Is Filled With Cracks, Madelyn Camrud

#60 Handmade Paper, Patricia Barone

#59 Under the Influence of Blackbirds, Sharon Van Sluys

#58 Jump Rope Queen, Karen Loeb

#57 Wolves, Jim Johnson

#56 The Second Thing I Remember, Judith Hougen

#55 Right by My Side, David Haynes (OP; e-book)

#54 Rumors from the Lost World, Alan Davis (e-book)

#53 Edith Jacobson Begins to Fly, Patricia Zontelli

#52 Learning to Dance & Other Stories, Sharon Oard Warner

#51 Mykonos: A Memoir , Nancy Raeburn (OP)

#50 Billy Brazil, Emilio DeGrazia (OP)

#49 House Fire: A Collection of Poems, B.J. Buhrow

#48 From the Lanai & Other Hawaii Stories, Jessica K. Saiki

#47 Pictures of Three Seasons, Gail Rixen

#46 Pieces from the Long Afternoon, Monica Ochtrup

#45 Primary Colors, Barbara Croft

#44 But I Won't Go Out in a Boat, Sharon Chmielarz

#43 No Peace at Versailles and Other Stories, Nina Barragan

#42 Borrowed Voices, Roger Sheffer

#41 This Body She's Entered, Mary K. Rummel

#40 Suburban Metaphysics, Ron Rindo
#39 Out Far, In Deep, Alvin Handelman
#38 Dismal River, Ronald Block
#37 Turning Out the Lights, Sigrid Bergie
#36 The Transparency of Skin, Catherine Stearns (OP)
#35 Burning the Prairie, John Reinhard
#34 Last Summer, Davida Kilgore (OP)
#33 The High Price of Everything, Kathleen Coskran
#32 Storm Lines, Warren Woessner (OP)
#31 Dying Old and Dying Young, Susan Williams
#30 Once, A Lotus Garden, Jessica Saiki (OP)
#28 The Wind, Patricia Barone
#27 All Manner of Monks, Benet Tvedten (OP)
#26 Flash Paper, Theresa Pappas (OP)
#25 Tap Dancing for Big Mom, Roseann Lloyd
#24 Twelve Below Zero, Anthony Bukoski (OP)
#23 Locomotion, Elizabeth Evans (OP)
#22 What I Cannot Say, I Will Say, Monica Ochtrup
#21 Descent of Heaven Over the Lake, Sheryl Noethe (OP)
#20 Matty's Heart, C.J. Hribal (OP)
#19 Stars Above, Stars Below, Margaret Hasse (OP)
#18 Golf Ball Diver, Neal Bowers (OP)
#17 The Weird Kid, Mark Vinz (OP)
#16 Morning Windows, Michael Moos (OP)
#15 Powers, Marisha Chamberlain (OP)
#14 Suspicious Origins, Perry Glasser (OP)
#13 Blenheim Palace, Wendy Parrish (OP)
#12 Rivers, Stories, Houses, Dreams, Madelon Sprengnether
#11 We'll Come When It Rains, Yvette Nelson (OP)
#10 Different Arrangements, Sharon Chmielarz
#9 Casualties, Katherine Carlson
#8 Night Sale, Richard Broderick
#7 When I Was a Father, Alvaro Carona-Hine (OP)

#6 Changing the Past, Laurie Taylor (OP)
#5 I Live in the Watchmaker's Town, Ruth Roston (OP)
#4 Normal Heart, Madelon Gohlke (OP)
#3 Heron Dancer, John Solensten
#2 The Reconstruction of Light, John Minczeski (OP)
#1 Household Wounds, Deborah Keenan (OP)